Yesterday's Wilderness Kingdom

Hier régnant désert

YVES BONNEFOY

TRANSLATED FROM THE FRENCH BY
ANTHONY RUDOLF

WITH A FOREWORD BY
JOHN E JACKSON

MPT BOOKS

2000

YESTERDAY'S
WILDERNESS KINGDOM
and
HIER RÉGNANT DÉSERT
bilingual edition

Cover design: Richard Hollis
Typesetting: WM Pank

ii institut français

This book is supported by the French Ministry for Foreign Affairs as part
of the Burgess Programme headed for the French Embassy in London by
the Institut Français du Royaume Uni.

MPT gratefully acknowledges the support of the Arts Council of England.

Representation and distribution in UK:
Signature Book Representation
Sunhouse, 2 Little Peter Street, Manchester M15 4PS
Distributed by Littlehampton Book Services
tel 01903 828800, fax 01903 828801

ISBN: 0 9533824 5 1

MPT BOOKS
School of Humanities
King's College London
Strand
London WC2R 2LS

CONTENTS

FOREWORD

JOHN E JACKSON

Yves Bonnefoy's relationship to *Hier régnant désert* (1958), now trans-
lated as *Yesterday's Wilderness Kingdom*, is an uneasy one. Of all his
poetry books, this is the only one he has ever attempted to modify
(however slightly) in later editions. The uneasiness is best explained,
perhaps, by the volume's position in the development of his work. It has
neither the abruptness of the near-Dionysian exultation of its predeces-
sor, *Du mouvement et de l'immobilité de Douve* (1953), nor the more serene
maturity of the book which followed it, *Pierre écrite* (1965). The latter is
the first of Bonnefoy's books to share King Lear's conviction that
'ripenesse is all'. But there are also more interior reasons. In his prose
meditation, *L'Arrière-pays* (1972), Bonnefoy states that the years during
which he composed *Hier régnant désert* were his 'darkest seasons', and
that the moral voice which resounds in some of its poems is there to
reproach the still young poet for having forsaken his holy grail, which
he names 'presence', and for having sacrificed it on the altar of formal
perfection. Bonnefoy, retrospectively, must have been somewhat impa-
tient with a volume whose major function in his eyes may have been to
give way to what was to come.

To us, however, *Hier régnant désert* may hold a different appeal. True,
its verse does not have the tension of the poetic prose in *Douve* or of the
verse in the more innovative later volumes. The recourse to the alexan-
drine, and what is more to partly rhymed alexandrines, signals a return
to more traditional and more conventional poetic form. But then not
only do these alexandrines convey a highly specific music which has its
own fascination – the music of a poet clearly heir to France's Mallarmean
and post-Mallarmean tradition – they also allow us to understand better
how the struggle for form is at the same time a struggle for meaning.
Indeed one could argue that this struggle is the central theme of the
book. The moral voice which makes itself heard in so many poems
addresses its reproach to the poet for abandoning the quest for the
hidden, for that which only poetic labour will uncover:

Why did you allow brambles to cover
That high silence you'd arrived at? . . .   (p.16)

It does not matter to you any more
That stone conceals the dark church, and that trees
Conceal the dazzled face of a redder sun . . .   (p.17)

A sort of moral ataraxy is blamed on the quest-bearer whose sin appears to be that he has surrendered to discouragement. It is, however, easy to guess that the reproach, though formulated in moral terms, is at the same time a poetic one; that, in other words, the poet is reproaching himself for his lack of boldness. And thus the answer to the reproach will be both a thematic one – negativity as such must be accepted, must be endured, however disheartening it may be – and a formal one: the emergence of a kind of poetry in which the alexandrine, though it still dominates, is gladly sacrificed to the necessity of a more urgent line:

> It was like tilling hard soil,
> That naked moment, torn, you feel the blade
> Thrusting into the very heart of darkness
> And you invent death
> Under a changing sky.   (p.50)

> And so it was
> A voice asked for trust, and still it turned
> Against itself, and still it made
> Of weariness its grandeur and its proof.   (p.34)

In what is one of the two most explicitly self-reflexive poems in the book, 'Imperfection is the Summit' (p.36), Bonnefoy goes so far as to allow himself an opening line of fifteen syllables and to conclude with a heptasyllabic line, while writing the others in real alexandrines.

Much the same can be said of Bonnefoy's lexical choices. Whereas no other book of his displays a more comprehensive use of traditional poetic symbols (fire, wind, church, bird, angel, light, oil etc) – a use perhaps related to the fact that at the time he was co-translating into modern French (with Albert Béguin) *La Quête du Saint Graal* – several of the poems, including some of the most convincing ones, do not hesitate to introduce a notable anti-classical vocabulary, such as the first stanza of 'Iron Bridge':

> No doubt there is still at the far end of a long street
> Where I walked as a child a pool of oil,
> Rectangle of heavy death under black sky.   (p.30)

In fact, as may be inferred from 'A Voice' (p.61), the poem whose tenth line gives its title to the volume, one suspects that the problem which lies at the core of the book is that of time. The exultant nature of the figure of Douve went hand in hand with her location in instantaneity. What Bonnefoy appears to have discovered after *Douve* is that instantaneity, though perhaps the most intensely exciting mode of time, still leaves the human being to address the problem of time in its ongoing mode, namely duration. The reproaches we have already referred to are the summons of a voice reproaching the poet for having allowed duration to become, exclusively, the negative counterweight to the instant:

> For you it is enough
> To take a long time dying as in sleep,
> And now you do not even love
> The shadow you will wed. (p.17)

Duration is seen as synonymous with timelessness and time is equated with an indefinite apathy verging on death. Conversely, it is only the fact that duration is opposed to the Dionysian instant which gives it a negative connotation. Time, and this is the great lesson of *Hier régnant désert*, also presupposes the 'nouvel amour', the new love, on condition that time is seen for what it is: trial by ordeal ('l'ordalie') the quest-bearer must undergo, the negative he must endure, inevitable darkness leading to new light. It is therefore appropriate that one of the poems where this lesson is figured is a poem which, I believe, stages the return of the voice of Douve, a voice which, however, is henceforth aware of the necessity of time:

> Hear me come alive again, I shall lead you
> Into the garden of presence,
> Abandoned at evening, overcast by shadows,
> Where, in this new love, your home is found.
>
> In yesterday's wilderness kingdom I
> Was a wild leaf, and free to die.
> But time was ripening, black moan in the valleys,
> The wound of water in the stones of day. (p.61)

'The wound of water' ('La blessure de l'eau') emerges here as the gift of a maturing time in contrast to the immobility of a 'yesterday', a frozen moment of the past whose solitary reign, while allowing the voice to die, ignored the voice's more arduous task: that of confronting life's uncertainties. The recurring image of the voice which resumes its song after limping into silence symbolises in the clearest way the movement we have described:

> Later I heard the other song awakened
> In the gloomy depth of the silent bird's song. (p.48)

If death is the ultimate ordeal every person must endure, *Hier régnant désert* helps us understand that beyond the ecstatic dying of Douve, there is another, a more mature way of coping with this ordeal, when we finally understand – in the words of TS Eliot in *Burnt Norton* – that 'only through time is time conquered'.

August 1999

TRANSLATOR'S NOTE

ANTHONY RUDOLF

The earliest drafts of some of these translations of Yves Bonnefoy's second book of poetry were made as long ago as 1963. Some versions appeared in print during the succeeding years: prematurely, my ear tells me after the event, after the process. About two years ago I decided to make an attempt at completing a translation of Bonnefoy's first three books of poetry rather than continue with my earlier practice, which had been to translate single poems from these and later books, as well as extracts from his prose.

I have now completed the latest revision of my earlier translations from *Yesterday's Wilderness Kingdom* [*Hier régnant désert*, 1958] – which was my first love among Bonnefoy's works and the second of the three books mentioned earlier – and have translated the handful of untranslated poems for the first time.

Earlier versions of some of these poems appeared in: *French Poetry Today* (edited by Edward Lucie-Smith and Simon Watson Taylor; Rapp and Whiting/André Deutsch), *The Random House Book of Twentieth Century French Poetry* (edited by Paul Auster), *New and Selected Poems of Yves Bonnefoy* (Carcanet/University of Chicago Press, 1995/6), *Things Dying Things Newborn*, a selection of Bonnefoy's poems translated and edited by myself (Menard Press, 1985), as was *Selected Poems of Yves Bonnefoy* (Jonathan Cape, 1968). *Things Dying Things Newborn* contains full acknowledgment of magazines which published translations from *Hier régnant désert* and other books by Bonnefoy. I would like to thank the editors and publishers of books and magazines which welcomed translations over the years – and also The Elephant Trust, whose grant bought and brought me joined-up time, at just the right moment, to work on the translations.

I would also like to thank six friends. Firstly, two poets: Gabriel Levin, who commented on various details in the latest manuscript, and Daniel Weissbort, who commented on the translation as a whole. Secondly, three scholars: Professor Norma Rinsler and Steven Jaron, whose comments just before the book went to press made me reconsider various workings (in one or two cases I was brought back full circle to solutions found in the earliest days) and Professor John Naughton. His fraternal generosity is remarkable, his book on Bonnefoy essential reading for all translators of this poet (*The Poetics of Yves Bonnefoy*, University of Chicago Press, 1984). Lastly, Yves Bonnefoy himself: 'words cannot express', to coin a phrase . . .

In preparing these final, or should I say latest, versions I have re-read not only Bonnefoy's own poetry and prose and some of the enormous amount of critical work on him published in French, English and other languages, but also translations of his poems, especially those by Galway Kinnell, John Naughton, Susanna Lang and Richard Pevear in English, and by Marc Grinberg in Russian.

Literary criticism and translation are both covered by the word interpretation. As a translator poet one is translating not only the original text but also – sometimes consciously, sometimes unconsciously – the interpretations or metatexts circulating around the sun of the original like so many planets. These have their place in the firmament of this poet's manifold *œuvre* for, as the Duc de La Rochefoucauld said, 'le soleil ni la mort ne se peuvent regarder fixement'. . .

Here I prefer to say nothing, in the prose of literary criticism, about Yves Bonnefoy's extraordinary and troubling book. Instead, I asked John E Jackson, author of an important work on Eliot, Celan and Bonnefoy (*La Question du moi*; La Baconnière / Payot, Neuchatel, 1978) and of the invaluable *Yves Bonnefoy* in the Seghers / Poètes d'aujourd'hui series (1976), to write an introduction.[1] This time round all my energies have gone into the other kind of interpretation, translation. But, as I have written elsewhere,[2] it was *this* very book, *Hier régnant désert*, found by chance in a Cambridge bookshop back in 1963, which changed my life. Over a period of thirty-seven years I have tried to introject its signs and wonders until it has become part of my own inner landscape, and then to project it back into the world, an English book at last. At the end of the work, this book, *Yesterday's Wilderness Kingdom* is, simply, a gift expressing my gratitude to another poet and another book, *Hier régnant désert*.

And so it was
A voice asked for trust, and still it turned
Against itself, and still it made
Of weariness its grandeur and its proof.

1.   In his Foreword, John E Jackson discusses Bonnefoy's use of alexandrines. I have not attempted to reproduce in English Yves Bonnefoy's alexandrines, perfect or modified, only their effect(s). For an excellent discussion of the problems in bringing across the effect(s) of a metre which is central to the poetic language which is being translated but not to one's own language, see Yves Bonnefoy's essay 'On the Translation of Form in Poetry' (*World Literature Today*, 53 / 3, Summer 1979), a magisterial rebuke to Joseph Brodsky's article of 7 February 1979 in the *New York Review of Books*. On the other hand (or foot?), Marianne Moore's versions of La Fontaine (*Selected Fables of La Fontaine*; Faber and Faber, 1955) and Ciaran Carson's Rimbaud, Baudelaire and Mallarmé in *The Alexandrine Plan* (Gallery Press 1998), both of which I came to late in the day, are worth thinking about in this context. I have myself touched on these issues in a few articles (see note 2).

2.   In the foreword to *New and Selected Poems of Yves Bonnefoy*, edited by John Naughton and myself and translated by Naughton, myself and others. I have also written on Yves Bonnefoy in a number of magazines, including *Agenda* 36 / 2 (1998) and the Bonnefoy issue of *Modern Poetry in Translation* (No 1, New Series, 1992). The *Agenda* article, slightly revised and reprinted in *In Other Words* 13-14 (Autumn-Winter 1999-2000), was my own translation of an article written in French and which was first published in the Yves Bonnefoy issue of *Le Temps qu'il fait*, 11, 1998. Finally there was my 1999 BBC Radio Three profile of Bonnefoy (produced by Michael Nangla).

Yesterday's Wilderness Kingdom

You want a world, said Diotima,
that is why you have everything – and nothing

HÖLDERLIN / *Hyperion*

THREATS OF THE WITNESS

THREATS OF THE WITNESS

I

What did you want to set up on this table
If not the double fire of our death?
Frightened, I destroyed in this world
The red, bare table where the dead wind speaks.

Then I grew older. Outside, the truth of words
And the truth of wind have ceased their fight.
The fire has drawn away, which was my church,
I am no longer even frightened, I do not sleep.

II

See, all the paths you went along are closed now,
No longer are you granted even the respite
To wander even lost. Earth, failing, sounds
With your footsteps which are going nowhere.

Why did you allow brambles to cover
That high silence you'd arrived at? The fire,
Empty, watches over memory's garden
And you, shadow in the shade, where are you, who are you?

III

You no longer come into this garden,
The paths of suffering and aloneness vanish,
The grasses intimate your face of death.

It does not matter to you any more
That stone conceals the dark church, and that trees
Conceal the dazzled face of a redder sun,

For you it is enough
To take a long time dying as in sleep,
And now you do not even love
The shadow you will wed.

IV

Despite these stars you are alone now,
The centre is far from you and near you,
You walked, you can walk, nothing changes now,
Always this same night which will never end.

See, you're separated from yourself now,
Always this same cry, but you do not hear it,
Are you dying, you who have no anguish now,
Are you even lost, you who seek after nothing?

V

The wind dies down, lord of the ancient sorrows,
Shall I be the last to take up arms for the dead?
Now the fire stirs only memory and ash,
Sound of a dead face, sound of a folded wing.

Do you consent to love only the iron of gray water
When the angel of your night closes the harbour
And loses in the still water of the harbour
Night's last glimmers caught in his dead wing?

Only suffer through the harshness of my words
And I shall conquer sleep and death for you,
For you I'll summon in the breaking tree
The flame that will be both your ship and harbour.

And raise the fire which has no place, no time,
Wind seeking fire, the summits of dead trees,
The horizon of a voice where stars are falling,
Moon merging with the chaos of the dead.

THE SOUND OF VOICES

Where is the sound of the voices that named you?
You are alone, enclosed with the dark boats.
As you walk upon this shifting ground, you have
A different song than this gray water in your heart,

A different hope than the departure now assured,
The dismal steps, the lantern swaying at the prow.
You do not love the river with its simple earthly waters,
Its moon-struck path where the wind subsides.

Rather, you say, rather on shores more dead,
The deep decay of palaces I was.
You love only the night as night, which bears
Your destiny: renunciation's torch.

SHORE OF ANOTHER DEATH

I

The bird that's freed itself from being Phoenix
Waits alone for death, up in the tree.
Wrapping itself in a night-time of wounds
It does not feel the sword go through its heart.

Like oil old and darkened in the lamps,
Like all the roads we were when lost,
Slowly it returns to the substance of the tree.

One day it will be,
One day it will know how to be, dead meat,
Throat-cut absence blood devours.

It will drop into grass, having found
In grass the deep structure of truth.
The taste of blood will beat in waves on its shore.

II

The bird will come apart through deepest want,
What was it but the voice that will not lie,
Through pride, and through instinct for non-being,
It will turn into the song of the dead.

It will grow old. A land of hard, bare forms
Will be the other face of that bird's voice.
Thus sand erodes a boat at rest beyond
The pull of tide and blackened in the wind.

It will be silent. Death is less severe. The bird
Will take, in the uselessness of being,
The few steps of a shadow whose wings were put
        to the sword.

It will know how it must die in gravest light
And thus the name of a light that is more joyous
Will be spoken, from another, darker world.

III

In the beginning there is sand, as it will be
The horrible end beneath the thrust of this cold wind.
When will these stars come to an end, you say,
Why are we heading into this cold space?

And why are we speaking such empty words,
Making our way as if night did not exist?
Better we hug the shoreline
And risk the threshold of a different coldness.

We were always on our way. Early lights
Carried the cold's majesty before us –
Little by little the long-seen coast
Named by words we did not know grew clearer.

SAN FRANCESCO IN THE EVENING

. . . And so the floor was marble in the dark
Room to which incurable hope had led you.
It might have been calm water where reflected
Lights carried the sounds of candles and evening away.

And yet no ship sought harbour there. No footstep
Troubled the water's stillness any more.
And so it is, I tell you, with our own mirages,
Heart's fun and games, eternal lights!

THE BEAUTIFUL SUMMER

Fire haunted our days and completed them,
Its blade wounded time with each grayer dawn.
The wind clashed with death on the roof over our beds.
The cold surrounded our hearts unceasingly.

It was a beautiful summer, dull, rending, dark,
You loved the sweetness of the summer showers
And you loved death which dominated summer
From the trembling pavilion of its ashy wings.

That year you were almost able to discern
A sign still black and brought to your attention
By the stones, the winds, the waters and the leaves.

And so the plough had started biting the loose earth
And your pride loved this new light,
The ecstasy of fear upon the summer earth.

Often in the silence of a ravine
I hear (or wish to hear, I do not know)
A body falling through the branches.
This blind fall that no cry ever
Interrupts or ends is long and slow.

Then I think how light traces a path through
The land where no one dies, no one is born.

TO A DEARTH

You'll know he keeps you in the dying hearth,
You'll know he's speaking to you as he mingles
Your body's ashes with the cold of dawn,
You'll know he is alone and unappeased.

He who has destroyed so much, who can no longer
Tell his silence from his nothingness,
Sees you, cruel dawn, arrive in darkness,
Burning long on the desert of the tables.

THE MORTAL FACE

Day leans over the river of the past,
It seeks to recover
Weapons lost early on,
Jewels of deep, childlike death.

It does not dare to know
If truly it is day
And if it has just cause to love those dawn words
Which for its sake have breached the walls of light.

A torch is carried into the gray of daylight.
Fire tears the light apart.
Thus the transparence of the flame
Bitterly denies the day.

And so the lamp was burning low,
Bending its gray face towards you,
Trembling, in the space of the trees,
Like a wounded bird laden with death.
Will the oil breaking in the harbours of
The ashen sea grow crimson one last day,
Will the ship, heading for shore through friendly foam,
Appear at last beneath the night's last star?

Here stone reigns alone, its soul enormous, gray
And you, you kept on walking, and still there was no day.

IRON BRIDGE

No doubt there is still at the far end of a long street
Where I walked as a child a pool of oil,
Rectangle of heavy death under black sky.

Since then, poetry
Has kept its waters apart from other waters,
No beauty no colour can retain it –
It suffers from iron and night.

It nourishes
A dead shore's long grief, an iron bridge
Flung towards the other even darker shore
Is its only real love, its only memory.

THE WATCHERS

I

There was a passage at the far end of the garden,
I dreamed that I was walking down this passage.
Death approached with his tall withered flowers,
I dreamed I took the black bouquet from him.

In my bedroom were some shelves.
I entered at nightfall
And saw two shrivelled women crying out
Up there on the black painted wood.

There was a staircase, and I dreamed
A dog howled in the middle of the night
In that place of no dog, and I saw
A dreadful white dog step out of the shadow.

II

Frightened, I waited. I watched out for him,
Perhaps at last a door was open
(Thus sometimes in broad daylight
A lamp kept on burning in the room,
I have loved nothing but this shore).

Ah death: he was the very image
Of a great empty harbour, and I knew
Past and future in his greedy eyes
Would continue to destroy each other
Like the sea and the sand on the shore,

And all the same I would create in him
The sad place of a song I bore
Like the mud and shadows I made into
Images of absence, when sea waters
Came to cleanse the shores of bitterness.

BEAUTY

She who ruins being, beauty,
Shall be tortured, broken on the wheel,
Dishonoured, found guilty, made into blood
And cry, and night, of all joy dispossessed –
O you, torn apart on iron gates before the dawn,
O you, trampled on every road and pierced,
Our high despair shall be to see you live,
Our heart that you may suffer, and our voice
To humiliate you in your tears, to name you
Liar, procuress of the darkened sky,
Yet your crippled body is our object of desire,
Our pity this heart leading only to mire.

TRIAL BY ORDEAL

I

I was the one who walks out of concern
For a late troubled water. It was lovely
That brightest of summers. It had been night
Always, unending, and forever.

In the clay of the seas
The foam's chrysanthemum, and there was still
That same stale earthy November smell
As I trod the black garden of the dead.

And so it was
A voice asked for trust, and still it turned
Against itself, and still it made
Of weariness its grandeur and its proof.

II

I don't know if I've conquered. But I've grasped
With a will the sword stuck in the stone.
I've spoken in the sword's night, and I've risked
Sense and beyond all sense the cold world.

For a moment all failed,
No longer did the red knife-edge of being
Pierce the gray shadow of the spoken word,
But at last the fire blazed forth,
The most violent of ships
Entered harbour.

Dawn of a second day,
At last I've come into your burning house
And broken this bread where distant water flows.

IMPERFECTION IS THE SUMMIT

There was this:
You had to destroy, destroy, destroy.
There was this:
Salvation is only found at such a price.

You had to
Ruin the naked face that rises in the marble,
Hammer at every beauty every form,

Love perfection because it is the threshold
But deny it once known, once dead forget it,

Imperfection is the summit.

VENERANDA

The orant is alone in the low and ill-lit room
Her dress is coloured like the dead in waiting,
The softest blue found in the world,
Flaked, revealing the ochre of bare stones.
Childhood is lonely, those who come are indistinct,
They lean across her body with their lamps.
Are you asleep? Your unslakeable presence burns
Like a soul, in these words I bring you once again.

You are alone, you have grown old in this room,
You are busy with the works of time and death.
But see, a low voice only has to tremble
For dawn to stream through windows once again.

A VOICE

I kept a fire going in the ordinary night
And now my words are purified through fire,
I kept watch, bright Fate, less anxious daughter
Of a dark and brooding Fate along the walls.

I had a little time to understand, to be,
I was the ghost, I loved not going out,
And I would wait, I was the patience of the rooms,
I knew the fire was not burning in vain . . .

VENERANDA

I

He comes, he is the gesture of a statue,
He speaks, his empire is of the dead,
Gigantic, he participates in stone,
Itself the sky of the anger of the dead.

He grasps, brings close and holds up to his face,
Lamp which will burn in the land of the dead,
The tiny orant's body bent and weeping
Which he protects from anguish and from death.

II

He leans over. May your hands guiding the impatient
Fire be desert, another world of cinder.
He shapes your hands into a room with ghostly windows
Where the fire shall break into rosaceous cinder.

He leans over you. Solemn, intent,
His face is gray while he reveres the fire,
His blood touches the weeping orant's teeth,
Big cold teeth, open to the rape of fire.

III

He comes, age dancing attendance. Because he looks at you
He sees his death which declares itself in you.
He is happy being threatened by the good you are.
Look, he is sleeping under your tall cold trees.

Trusting, he sleeps. May your anxious desire
Not to wake him be a tree that no one fears.
– Tree, however, where the flame's already soared,
Table where your gift takes hold, overflows, consumes.

A VOICE

Nettle, oh prow of this shore where he breaks,
You standing there frozen in the wind,
Make me the sign of presence, oh my maidservant,
In your black flaked dress.

Oh gray stone,
If it is true you have the colour of blood
Be moved by this blood which goes right through you,
Open up for me the harbour of your cry,

That through you I may approach
The one pretending to sleep,
His head shadowing yours.

VENERANDA

He is another land, divides from her.
Nothing will bring together these strange worlds,
Not even this fire miming in the hearth
The greater fire which shines on empty worlds.

It matters little that a man has found his way
Into dreams, has broken ancient chains.
Long was this night. So many years revolved
Around the sombre garden of the seas.

ALL NIGHT

All night the beast has moved about the room,
What is this road that does not want to end?
All night the boat has sought the river bank,
What are these absent wanting to come back?
All night the sword has coupled with the wound,
What is this pain that seizes on no thing?
All night the beast has groaned within the room,
Has stained with blood, denied the light of rooms,
What is this death that heals nothing at all?

You will lie down upon the simple earth,
Who told you it belonged to you?

The wandering light of the unchanged sky
Will begin eternal morning once again.

You'll think you're reborn in the dead of night,
The fire renounced, the fire nearly out.

But the angel will come with his hands of ash
To smother this ardour which has no end.

MEMORY

And so it was: the fingers were clenched.
They took the place of memory.
The sorrowful guardian forces had to be loosened
To throw off the ocean and the tree.

THE SONG OF SAFEGUARD

Let the bird be torn to sand, you said,
Let him, high in his dawn sky, be our shore.
But he, shipwreck of the singing heavens, weeping
Was already falling into the clay of the dead.

The bird called me; I obeyed the summons,
Agreed I would live in this evil room.
Again I said it was my heart's desire,
I yielded to the dead sound moving inside me.

Then I fought, made words I was obsessed by
Appear clear-cut on the window, cold like myself.
The bird sang on, his voice was cruel, black
And I detested night a second time.

I grew old, now passion, bitter nightwatch,
I called forth a silence in which I was invisible.
Later I heard the other song awakened
In the gloomy depth of the silent bird's song.

LEAVES ILLUMINED

I

You say he stood there, on the other shore,
And at the close of day watched out for you?

The bird in the tree of silence had seized our hearts
With his great and simple and eager song,
He led
All voices down the night where voices vanish
With their real words,
And the words flutter among the leaves,
Still calling out, still loving vainly
Whatever is lost,
The tall grief-laden ship
Took all irony
Far from our shore, this was the angel
Of leaving the land of hearths and lamps,
Of yielding to the foamy taste of night.

II

The voice was pure irony among the trees,
Was distance, death,
Release of dawns far from us

In a rejected place. And our harbour
Was black clay. No ship
Had ever shown a sign of light there,
All began with this song of a cruel dawn,
A hope which redeems, a poverty.

It was like tilling hard soil,
That naked moment, torn, you feel the blade
Thrusting into the very heart of darkness
And you invent death
Under a changing sky.

III

But among the trees,
In the flame of fruit barely glimpsed,
The sword of red and blue kept probing
The primal wound
Deeply suffered, then forgotten when night came.

The angel of living here, arriving late,
Was torn like a dress among the trees,
His feet of leaves appeared beneath the lamps
As matter, motion and night.

IV

He is the earth, the earth is dark, where you must live,
You shall not deny the stones of this home,
Your shadow will stretch out beside the mortal shadows
On flagstones visited then abandoned by daylight.

He is the ground of dawn. Where an essential shadow
Veils every light and every truth.
But even an exile loves the earth he stands on
So true it is that *amor vincit omnia*.

INFIRMITY OF FIRE

The fire has caught, that is the destiny of branches,
It will touch their heart of cold and broken stones;
This fire which entered the harbour of all things born
Will come to rest upon the shores of matter.

It will burn. But, pointlessly, as you know well,
No-man's land will show beneath the flames,
The star of badlands will spread beneath the flames,
The star of death will light up all our roads.

It will grow old. The ford where shadows crowd
Sparkles only briefly as it passes
And the Idea breaks through matter it consumes
And renounces time it fails to redeem.

At last you will hear
The bird's cry, like a sword
Far off, on the mountain wall
And you will know a sign was carved
On the hilt, at the place of hope and light.
You will appear
On the parvis of the cry of the swaying bird,
Here all waiting ends, you understand,
Here in the immemorial grass you will see
The naked blade that you must grasp aglow.

TO THE VOICE OF KATHLEEN FERRIER

All softness and irony assembled
For a farewell of crystal and haze.
The sword's deep thrusts were near silent,
The light of the blade was obscured.

I praise this voice mingled with gray
Wavering in the distance of the song which died away
As if beyond pure forms there trembled
Another song, the only absolute.

O light and light's nothingness, O you tears
Smiling higher than anguish or hope,
O swan, real place in unreal dark waters,
O wellspring in the very deep of evening!

It seems you know well the two shores:
Deep sorrow, high joy.
Over there, in the light among the dark reeds
It seems that you draw from eternity.

LAND OF MORNING TWILIGHT

Dawn crosses the threshold, the wind now is silent.
The fire has withdrawn into the hive of shadows.

Land of cold mouths, you cry out
This most ancient mourning through your secret gullies,
Dawn will flower again upon your eyes in sleep,
Reveal to me your orant's face, defiled.

THE RAVINE

There was this:
A sword had been driven
Into the mass of stone.
The hilt was rusted, the ancient blade
Had reddened the flank of the gray stone.
And you had, you knew, to grasp
So much absence with both hands, and tear
The dark flame from its vein of night.
Words were engraved in the blood of the stone:
They gave directions: knowledge then death.

Enter the ravine of absence, then move on,
Here, amid the rubble, is the harbour.
The song of a bird
Will point it out to you on the new shore.

ETERNITY OF FIRE

Phoenix speaking to fire, which is destiny
And the bright landscape casting shadows,
I am the one you're waiting for, he says,
I come to vanish in your solemn country.

He stares at the fire, the fire's beginnings,
Sees how it finds its place in a soul's dark,
And when dawn appears at windows, how
The fire goes dead, and sleeps deeper than fire.

He nourishes it with silence. He hopes
Each fold of an eternal silence,
Settling over it like sand,
Will aggravate its immortality.

You will know a bird has spoken, higher
Than any real tree, more simply
Than any voice at home among our branches,
And you will do your best to leave the harbour
Of these ashen or stony trees, your cries of old.

You will walk,
For a long time your steps will be the night, bare earth,

And the bird will move away singing from shore to shore.

TO A LAND OF DAWN

Dawn, daughter of tears, restore the room
– Peaceable gray kingdom once again –
And the heart, where order had ruled. So much night
Required of this fire that it wane and die.
We must keep vigil over the dead face.
It has hardly changed . . . The ship of lamps,
Will it reach the port it most desired,
Turned to ashes on these tables, will the flame
Spread elsewhere into a different brightness?
Dawn, raise up, hold the face without shadow,
Colour bit by bit time starting round again.

A VOICE

Hear me come alive again in these forests
Under memory's branches
Where green I pass by,
Burnt smile of ancient plants upon the earth,
Coal born of daylight.

Hear me come alive again, I shall lead you
Into the garden of presence,
Abandoned at evening, overcast by shadows,
Where, in this new love, your home is found.

In yesterday's wilderness kingdom I
Was a wild leaf, and free to die.
But time was ripening, black moan in the valleys,
The wound of water in the stones of day.

VENERANDA

O, what fire is in this broken bread,
How pure the dawn amid the fading stars!
I see daylight arrive among the stones,
White it surrounds you, alone and dressed in black.

How many stars will have crossed
The always deniable earth?
But you yourself have kept the torch
Of an ancient freedom alight.

Earth-bound, like great trees,
You have the strength
To be tied down here, but free
Among the highest winds.

Just as impatient birth
Fissures dry earth
Your eyes refuse
The weight of clay stars.

Calm now, do you remember
The time when we clashed like two armies,
What remained in our hearts
But desire unending for oblivion?

We had not passed through the only gate,
At evening or wisdom to live a life
Found in grisaille, in the acanthus of the dead.

We had not loved
The long night's fire, the unwearying patience
Which turns all dead boughs into dawn for us.

THAT DISCOVERED COUNTRY

Star on the threshold. Wind, held
In motionless hands.
Speech and wind had fought and fought,
And then the sudden silence of the wind.

That discovered country was all gray stone.
Far off, deep down, a no river's light shone.
But the rains of night on the surprised earth
Have awakened the ardour you name time.

DELPHI, THE SECOND DAY

Here the unquiet voice agrees to love
Simple stone,
Flagstones time enslaves, delivers.
The olive tree whose strength tastes of dry stone.

The footstep in its true place. The unquiet voice
Happy beneath the rocks of silence,
The infinite, the undefined responsory
Of death, shore, sheep-bells. Your bright abyss
Inspired no awe, Delphi on the second day.

HERE, FOREVER HERE

Here, in the bright place. It is no longer dawn
But daytime with its sayable desires.
Of a song's mirages in your dream there is
Only this flashing of stones to come.

Here, until evening. The rose of shadows
Will turn upon the walls. The rose of hours
Will shed its petals without noise. The marble floor
Will command our steps so much in love with daylight.

Here, forever here. Stones and more stones
Have built the land spoken by memory.
Still the sound of simple falling fruit
Barely fires time in you, time which will heal.

The voice of what destroys
Still sounds in the stone tree,
The step risked at the gate
May yet conquer the night.

Whence Oedipus, passing by?
But look, he has prevailed.
Inflexible wisdom scatters
As soon as he replies.

The Sphinx who keeps silent remains
In the sand of the Idea,
But speaks at last, and succumbs.

Why words? Because of trust,
And that a fire shall again pass through
The voice of Oedipus, saved.

THE SAME VOICE, ALWAYS

I am like the bread you will break,
The fire you will make, the pure water
That will take you through the land of the dead.

Like the foam
Which has ripened for you light and harbour.

Like the bird of evening which effaces the shores,
Like the evening wind, suddenly rougher and cold.

THE BIRD OF THE RUINS

The bird of the ruins separates from death,
Makes its nest in gray stone beneath the sun
And passing through all memory and sorrow
No longer knows what morrow is, only eternity.

Hier régnant désert

Tu veux un monde, dit Diotima.
C'est pourquoi tu as tout, et tu n'as rien.

Hyperion

MENACES DU TÉMOIN

MENACES DU TÉMOIN

I

Que voulais-tu dresser sur cette table,
Sinon le double feu de notre mort?
J'ai eu peur, j'ai détruit dans ce monde la table
Rougeâtre et nue, où se déclare le vent mort.

Puis j'ai vieilli. Dehors, vérité de parole
Et vérité de vent ont cessé leur combat.
Le feu s'est retiré, qui était mon église,
Je n'ai même plus peur, je ne dors pas.

II

Vous, déjà tous chemins que tu suivais se ferment,
Il ne t'est plus donné même ce répit
D'aller même perdu. Terre qui se dérobe
Est le bruit de tes pas qui ne progressent plus.

Pourquoi as-tu laissé les ronces recouvrir
Un haut silence où tu étais venu?
Le feu veille désert au jardin de mémoire
Et toi, ombre dans l'ombre, où es-tu, qui es-tu?

III

Tu cesses de venir dans ce jardin,
Les chemins de souffrir et d'être seul s'effacent,
Les herbes signifient ton visage mort.

Il ne t'importe plus que soient cachés
Dans la pierre l'église obscure, dans les arbres
Le visage aveuglé d'un plus rouge soleil,

Il te suffit
De mourir longuement comme en sommeil,
Tu n'aimes même plus l'ombre que tu épouses.

IV

Tu es seul maintenant malgré ces étoiles,
Le centre est près de toi et loin de toi,
Tu as marché, tu peux marcher, plus rien ne change,
Toujours la même nuit qui ne s'achève pas.

Et vois, tu es déjà séparé de toi-même,
Toujours ce même cri, mais tu ne l'entends pas,
Es-tu celui qui meurt, toi qui n'as plus d'angoisse,
Es-tu même perdu, toi qui ne cherches pas?

V

Le vent se tait, seigneur de la plus vieille plainte,
Serai-je le dernier qui s'arme pour les morts?
Déjà le feu n'est plus que mémoire et que cendre
Et bruit d'aile fermée, bruit de visage mort.

Consens-tu de n'aimer que le fer d'une eau grise
Quand l'ange de ta nuit viendra clore le port
Et qu'il perdra dans l'eau immobile du port
Les dernières lueurs dans l'aile morte prises?

Oh, souffre seulement de ma dure parole
Et pour toi je vaincrai le sommeil et la mort,
Pour toi j'appellerai dans l'arbre qui se brise
La flamme qui sera le navire et le port.

Pour toi j'élèverai le feu sans lieu ni heure,
Un vent cherchant le feu, les cimes du bois mort,
L'horizon d'une voix où les étoiles tombent
Et la lune mêlée au désordre des morts.

LE BRUIT DES VOIX

Le bruit des voix s'est tu, qui te désignait.
Tu es seul dans l'enclos des barques obscures.
Marches-tu sur ce sol qui bouge, mais tu as
Un autre chant que cette eau grise dans ton coeur,

Un autre espoir que ce départ que l'on assure
Ces pas mornes, ce feu qui chancelle à l'avant.
Tu n'aimes pas le fleuve aux simples eaux terrestres
Et son chemin de lune où se calme le vent.

Plutôt, dis-tu, plutôt sur de plus mortes rives,
Des palais que je fus le haut délabrement.
Tu n'aimes que la nuit en tant que nuit, qui porte
La torche, ton destin, de tout renoncement.

RIVE D'UNE AUTRE MORT

I

L'oiseau qui s'est dépris d'être Phénix
Demeure seul dans l'arbre pour mourir.
Il s'est enveloppé de la nuit de blessure,
Il ne sent pas l'épée qui pénètre son cœur.

Comme l'huile a vieilli et noirci dans les lampes,
Comme tant de chemins que nous étions, perdus,
Il fait un lent retour à la matière d'arbre.

Il sera bien un jour,
Il saura bien un jour être la bête morte,
L'absence au col tranché que dévore le sang.

Il tombera dans l'herbe, ayant trouvé
Dans l'herbe le profond de toute vérité,
Le goût du sang battra de vagues son rivage.

II

L'oiseau se défera par misère profonde,
Qu'était-il que la voix qui ne veut pas mentir,
Il sera par orgueil et native tendance
A n'être que néant, le chant des morts.

Il vieillira. Pays aux formes nues et dures
Sera l'autre versant de cette voix.
Ainsi noircit au vent des sables de l'usure
La barque retirée où le flot ne va pas.

Il se taira. La mort est moins grave. Il fera
Dans l'inutilité d'être les quelques pas
De l'ombre dont le fer a déchiré les ailes.

Il saura bien mourir dans la grave lumière
Et ce sera parler au nom d'une lumière
Plus heureuse, établie dans l'autre monde obscur.

III

Le sable est au début comme il sera
L'horrible fin sous la poussée de ce vent froid.
Où est le bout, dis-tu, de tant d'étoiles,
Pourquoi avançons-nous dans ce lieu froid?

Et pourquoi disons-nous d'aussi vaines paroles,
Allant et comme si la nuit n'existait pas?
Mieux vaut marcher plus près de la ligne d'écume
Et nous aventurer au seuil d'un autre froid.

Nous venions de toujours. De hâtives lumières
Portaient au loin pour nous la majesté du froid
– Peu à peu grandissait la côte longtemps vue
Et dite par des mots que nous ne savions pas.

A SAN FRANCESCO, LE SOIR

. . . Ainsi le sol était de marbre dans la salle
Obscure, où te mena l'inguérissable espoir.
On eût dit d'une eau calme où de doubles lumières
Portaient au loin les voix des cierges et du soir.

Et pourtant nul vaisseau n'y demandait rivage,
Nul pas n'y troublait plus la quiétude de l'eau.
Ainsi, te dis-je, ainsi de nos autres mirages,
O fastes dans nos cœurs, ô durables flambeaux !

LE BEL ÉTÉ

Le feu hantait nos jours et les accomplissait,
Son fer blessait le temps à chaque aube plus grise,
Le vent heurtait la mort sur le toit de nos chambres,
Le froid ne cessait pas d'environner nos cœurs.

Ce fut un bel été, fade, brisant et sombre,
Tu aimas la douceur de la pluie en été
Et tu aimas la mort qui dominait l'été
Du pavillon tremblant de ses ailes de cendre.

Cette année-la, tu vins à presque distinguer
Un signe toujours noir devant tes yeux porté
Par les pierres, les vents, les eaux et les feuillages.

Ainsi le soc déjà mordait la terre meuble
Et ton orgueil aima cette lumière neuve,
L'ivresse d'avoir peur sur la terre d'été.

Souvent dans le silence d'un ravin
J'entends (ou je désire entendre, je ne sais)
Un corps tomber parmi des branches. Longue et lente
Est cette chute aveugle; que nul cri
Ne vient jamais interrompre ou finir.

Je pense alors aux processions de la lumière
Dans le pays sans naître ni mourir.

A UNE PAUVRETÉ

Tu sauras qu'il te tient dans l'âtre qui s'achève,
Tu sauras qu'il te parle, et remuant
Les cendres de ton corps avec le froid de l'aube,
Tu sauras qu'il est seul et ne s'apaise pas.

Lui qui a tant détruit; qui ne sait plus
Distinguer son néant de son silence,
Il te voit, aube dure, en ténèbre venir
Et longuement brûler sur le désert des tables.

LE VISAGE MORTEL

Le jour se penche sur le fleuve du passé,
Il cherche à ressaisir
Les armes tôt perdues,
Les joyaux de la mort enfantine profonde.

Il n'ose pas savoir
S'il est vraiment le jour
Et s'il a droit d'aimer cette parole d'aube
Qui a troué pour lui la muraille du jour.

Une torche est portée dans le jour gris.
Le feu déchire le jour.
Il y a que la transparence de la flamme
Amèrement nie le jour.

Il y a que la lampe brûlait bas,
Qu'elle penchait vers toi sa face grise,
Qu'elle tremblait, dans l'espace des arbres,
Comme un oiseau blessé chargé de mort.
– L'huile brisant aux ports de la mer cendreuse
Va-t-elle s'empourprer d'un dernier jour,
Le navire qui veut l'écume puis la rive
Paraîtra-t-il enfin sous l'étoile du jour?

Ici la pierre est seule et d'âme vaste et grise
Et toi tu as marché sans que vienne le jour.

LE PONT DE FER

Il y a sans doute toujours au bout d'une longue rue
Où je marchais enfant une mare d'huile,
Un rectangle de lourde mort sous le ciel noir.

Depuis la poésie
A séparé ses eaux des autres eaux,
Nulle beauté nulle couleur ne la retiennent,
Elle s'angoisse pour du fer et de la nuit.

Elle nourrit
Un long chagrin de rive morte, un pont de fer
Jeté vers l'autre rive encore plus nocturne
Est sa seule mémoire et son seul vrai amour.

LES GUETTEURS

I

Il y avait un couloir au fond du jardin,
Je rêvais que j'allais dans ce couloir,
La mort venait aves ses fleurs hautes flétries,
Je rêvais que je lui prenais ce bouquet noir.

Il y avait une étagère dans ma chambre,
J'entrais au soir,
Et je voyais deux femmes racornies
Crier debout sur le bois peint de noir.

Il y avait un escalier, et je rêvais
Qu'au mileu de la nuit un chien hurlait
Dans cet espace de nul chien, et je voyais
Un horrible chien blanc sortir de l'ombre.

II

J'attendais, j'avais peur, je la guettais,
Peut-être enfin une porte s'ouvrait
(Ainsi parfois dans la salle durait
Dans le plein jour une lampe allumée,
Je n'ai jamais aimé que cette rive).

Était-elle la mort, elle ressemblait
A un port vaste et vide, et je savais
Que dans les yeux avides le passé
Et l'avenir toujours se détruiraient
Comme le sable et la mer sur la rive,

Et qu'en elle pourtant j'établirais
Le lieu triste d'un chant que je portais
Comme l'ombre et la boue dont je faisais
Des images d'absence quand venait
L'eau effacer l'amertume des rives.

LA BEAUTÉ

Celle qui ruine l'être, la beauté,
Sera suppliciée, mise à la roue,
Déshonorée, dite coupable, faite sang
Et cri, et nuit, de toute joie dépossédée
– O déchirée sur toutes grilles d'avant l'aube,
O piétinée sur toute route et traversée,
Notre haut désespoir sera que tu vives,
Notre cœur que tu souffres, notre voix
De t'humilier parmi tes larmes, de te dire
La menteuse, la pourvoyeuse du ciel noir,
Notre désir pourtant étant ton corps infirme,
Notre pitié ce cœur menant à toute boue.

L'ORDALIE

I

J'étais celui qui marche par souci
D'une eau dernière trouble. Il faisait beau
Dans l'été le plus clair. Il faisait nuit
De toujours et sans borne et pour toujours.

Dans la glaise des mers
Le chrysanthème de l'écume et c'était toujours
La même odeur terreuse et fade de novembre
Quand je foulais le noir jardin des morts.

Il y avait
Qu'une voix demandait d'être crue, et toujours
Elle se retournait contre soi et toujours
Faisait de se tarir sa grandeur et sa preuve.

II

Je ne sais pas si je suis vainqueur. Mais j'ai saisi
D'un grand cœur l'arme enclose dans la pierre.
J'ai parlé dans la nuit de l'arme, j'ai risqué
Le sens et au delà du sens le monde froid.

Un instant tout manqua,
Le fer rouge de l'être ne troua plus
La grisaille du verbe,
Mais enfin le feu se leva,
Le plus violent navire
Entra au port.

Aube d'un second jour,
Je suis enfin venu dans ta maison brûlante
Et j'ai rompu ce pain où l'eau lointaine coule.

L'IMPERFECTION EST LA CIME

Il y avait qu'il fallait détruire et détruire et détruire,
Il y avait que le salut n'est qu'à ce prix.

Ruiner la face nue qui monte dans le marbre,
Marteler toute forme toute beauté.

Aimer la perfection parce qu'elle est le seuil,
Mais la nier sitôt connue, l'oublier morte,

L'imperfection est la cime.

VENERANDA

L'orante est seule dans la salle basse très peu claire,
Sa robe a la couleur de l'attente des morts,
Et c'est le bleu le plus éteint qui soit au monde,
Écaillé, découvrant l'ocre des pierres nues.
L'enfance est seule, et ceux qui viennent sont obscurs,
Ils se penchent avec des lampes sur son corps.
Oh, dors-tu? Ta présence inapaisable brûle
Comme une âme, en ces mots que je t'apporte encor.

Tu es seule, tu as vieilli dans cette chambre,
Tu vaques aux travaux du temps et de la mort.
Vois pourtant, il suffit qu'une voix basse tremble
Pour que l'aube ruisselle aux vitres reparues.

UNE VOIX

J'entretenais un feu dans la nuit la plus simple,
J'usais selon le feu de mots désormais purs,
Je veillais, Parque claire et d'une Parque sombre
La fille moins anxieuse au rivage des murs.

J'avais un peu de temps pour comprendre et pour être,
J'étais l'ombre, j'aimais de garder le logis,
Et j'attendais, j'étais la patience des salles,
Je savais que le feu ne brûlait pas en vain . . .

VENERANDA

I

Il vient, il est le geste d'une statue,
Il parle, son empire est chez les morts,
Il est géant, il participe de la pierre,
Elle-même le ciel de colère des morts.

Il saisit. Il attire et tient sur son visage,
Lampe qui brûlera dans le pays des morts,
L'infime corps criant et ployé de l'orante,
Il le protège de l'angoisse et de la mort.

II

Il se penche. Désert selon quelque autre cendre
Que soient tes mains guidant l'impatience du feu.
Il forme de tes mains la salle aux vitres d'ombre
Où se déchirera la rosace du feu.

Il se penche sur toi. Et grave dans l'effort
Étant sa face grise adorante du feu,
Il touche de son sang les dents de la pleureuse,
Froides, larges, ouvertes aux violences du feu.

III

Il vient, et c'est vieillir. Parce qu'il te regarde,
Il regarde sa mort qui se déclare en toi.
Il aime que ce bien que tu es le menace,
Regarde-le dormir sous tes grands arbres froids.

Il a confiance, il dort. Arbre de peu d'alarme
Soit ton désir anxieux de ne l'éveiller pas.
– Arbre où pourtant d'un bond se fait déjà la flamme,
Table où le don saisit, comble, consumera.

UNE VOIX

Ortie, ô proue de ce rivage où il se brise,
O debout glacée dans le vent,
Fais-moi le signe de présence, ô ma servante
En robe noire écaillée.

O pierre grise,
S'il est vrai que tu aies la couleur du sang,
Émeus-toi de ce sang qui te traverse,
Ouvre-moi le port de ton cri,

Qu'en toi je vienne vers lui
Qui fait semblant de dormir
La tête close sur toi.

VENERANDA

Il se sépare d'elle, il est une autre terre,
Rien ne réunira ces globes étrangers
Et même pas ce feu qui imite dans l'âtre
Le feu plus grand qui luit sur les mondes déserts.

Comme il importe peu qu'un homme ait eu passage
Dans le rêve, ou rompu les plus antiques fers!
Longue fut cette nuit. Et tant d'années
Auront tourné sur le jardin sombre des mers.

TOUTE LA NUIT

Toute la nuit la bête a bougé dans la salle,
Qu'est-ce que ce chemin qui ne veut pas finir,
Toute la nuit la barque a cherché le rivage,
Qu'est-ce que ces absents qui veulent revenir,
Toute la nuit l'épée a connu la blessure,
Qu'est-ce que ce tourment qui ne sait rien saisir,
Toute la nuit la bête a gémi dans la salle,
Ensanglanté, nié la lumière des salles,
Qu'est-ce que cette mort qui ne va rien guérir?

Tu te coucheras sur la terre simple,
De qui tenais-tu qu'elle t'appartînt ?

Du ciel inchangé l'errante lumière
Recommencera l'éternel matin.

Tu croiras renaître aux heures profondes
Du feu renoncé, du feul mal éteint.

Mais l'ange viendra de ses mains de cendre
Étouffer l'ardeur qui n'a pas de fin.

LA MÉMOIRE

Il y a que les doigts s'étaient crispés,
Ils tenaient lieu de mémoire,
Il a fallu desceller les tristes forces gardiennes
Pour jeter l'arbre et la mer.

LE CHANT DE SAUVEGARDE

Que l'oiseau se déchire en sables, disais-tu,
Qu'il soit, haut dans son ciel de l'aube, notre rive.
Mais lui, le naufragé de la voûte chantante,
Pleurant déjà tombait dans l'argile des morts.

L'oiseau m'a appelé, je suis venu,
J'ai accepté de vivre dans la salle
Mauvaise, j'ai redit qu'elle était désirable,
J'ai cédé au bruit mort qui remuait en moi.

Puis j'ai lutté, j'ai fait que des mots qui m'obsèdent
Paraissent en clarté sur la vitre où j'eus froid.
L'oiseau chantait toujours de voix noire et cruelle,
J'ai détesté la nuit une seconde fois,

Et j'ai vieilli, passion désormais, âpre veille,
J'ai fait naître un silence où je me suis perdu.
– Plus tard j'ai entendu l'autre chant, qui s'éveille
Au fond morne du chant de l'oiseau qui s'est tu.

LE FEUILLAGE ÉCLAIRÉ

I

Dis-tu qu'il se tenait sur l'autre rive,
Dis-tu qu'il te guettait à la fin du jour?

L'oiseau dans l'arbre de silence avait saisi
De son chant vaste et simple et avide nos coeurs,
Il conduisait
Toutes voix dans la nuit où les voix se perdent
Avec leurs mots réels,
Avec le mouvement des mots dans le feuillage
Pour appeler encor, pour aimer vainement
Tout ce qui est perdu,
Le haut vaisseau chargé de douleur entraînait
Toute ironie loin de notre rivage,
Il était l'ange de quitter la terre d'âtres et de lampes
Et de céder au goût d'écume de la nuit.

II

La voix était d'ironie pure dans les arbres,
De distance, de mort,
De descellement d'aubes loin de nous

Dans un lieu refusé. Et notre port
Était de glaise noire. Nul vaisseau
N'y avait jamais fait le signe de lumière,
Tout commençait avec ce chant d'aube cruelle,
Un espoir qui délivre, une pauvreté.

C'était comme en labour de terre difficile
L'instant nu, déchiré
Où l'on sent que le fer trouve le cœur de l'ombre
Et invente la mort sous un ciel qui change.

III

Mais dans les arbres,
Dans la flamme des fruits à peine aperçue,
L'épée du rouge et du bleu
Durement maintenait la première blessure,
La soufferte puis l'oubliée quand vint la nuit.

L'ange de vivre ici, le tard venu,
Se déchirait comme une robe dans les arbres,
Ses jambes de feuillage sous les lampes
Paraissaient, par matière et mouvement et nuit.

IV

Il est la terre, elle l'obscure, où tu dois vivre,
Tu ne dénieras pas les pierres du séjour,
Ton ombre doit s'étendre auprès d'ombres mortelles
Sur les dalles où vient et ne vient pas le jour.

Il est la terre d'aube. Où une ombre essentielle
Voile toute lumière et toute vérité.
Mais même en lieu d'exil on a aimé la terre,
Tant il est vrai que rien ne peut vaincre l'amour.

L'INFIRMITÉ DU FEU

Le feu a pris, c'est là le destin des branches,
Il va toucher leur cœur de pierraille et de froid,
Lui qui venait au port de toute chose née,
Aux rives de matière il se reposera.

Il brûlera. Mais tu le sais, en pure perte,
L'espace d'un sol nu sous le feu paraîtra,
L'étoile d'un sol noir sous le feu s'étendra,
L'étoile de la mort éclairera nos routes.

Il vieillira. Le gué où buissonnent les ombres
N'aura étincelé qu'une heure, sous son pas.
L'Idée aussi franchit la matière qu'elle use
Et renonce à ce temps qu'elle ne sauve pas.

Tu entendras
Enfin ce cri d'oiseau, comme une épée
Au loin, sur la paroi de la montagne,
Et tu sauras qu'un signe fut gravé
Sur la garde, au point d'espérance et de lumière.
Tu paraîtras
Sur le parvis du cri de l'oiseau chancelant,
C'est ici que prend fin l'attente, comprends-tu,
Ici dans l'herbe ancienne tu verras
Briller le glaive nu qu'il te faut saisir.

A LA VOIX DE KATHLEEN FERRIER

Toute douceur toute ironie se rassemblaient
Pour un adieu de cristal et de brume,
Les coups profonds du fer faisaient presque silence,
La lumière du glaive s'était voilée.

Je célèbre la voix mêlée de couleur grise
Qui hésite aux lointains du chant qui s'est perdu
Comme si au delà de toute forme pure
Tremblât un autre chant et le seul absolu.

O lumière et néant de la lumière, ô larmes
Souriantes plus haut que l'angoisse ou l'espoir,
O cygne, lieu réel dans l'irréelle eau sombre,
O source, quand ce fut profondément le soir!

Il semble que tu connaisses les deux rives,
L'extrême joie et l'extrême douleur.
Là-bas, parmi ces roseaux gris dans la lumière,
Il semble que tu puises de l'éternel.

TERRE DU PETIT JOUR

L'aube passe le seuil, le vent s'est tu,
Le feu s'est retiré dans la laure des ombres.

Terre des bouches froides, ô criant
Le plus vieux deuil par tes secrètes clues,
L'aube va refleurir sur tes yeux de sommeil,
Découvre-moi souillé ton visage d'orante.

LE RAVIN

Il y a qu'une épée était engagée
Dans la masse de pierre.
La garde était rouillée, l'antique fer
Avait rougi le flanc de la pierre grise.
Et tu savais qu'il te fallait saisir
A deux mains tant d'absence, et arracher
A sa gangue de nuit la flamme obscure.
Des mots étaient gravés dans le sang de la pierre,
Ils disaient ce chemin, connaître puis mourir.

Entre dans le ravin d'absence, éloigne-toi,
C'est ici en pierrailles qu'est le port.
Un chant d'oiseau
Te le désignera sur la nouvelle rive.

L'ÉTERNITÉ DU FEU

Phénix parlant au feu, qui est destin
Et paysage clair jetant ses ombres,
Je suis celui que tu attends, dit-il,
Je viens me perdre en ton grave pays.

Il regarde le feu. Comment il vient,
Comment il s'établit dans l'âme obscure
Et quand l'aube paraît à des vitres, comment
Le feu se taît, et va dormir plus bas que feu.

Il le nourrit de silence. Il espère
Que chaque pli d'un silence éternel,
En se posant sur lui comme le sable,
Aggravera son immortalité.

Tu sauras qu'un oiseau a parlé, plus haut
Que tout arbre réel, plus simplement
Que toute voix d'ici dans nos ramures,
Et tu t'efforceras de quitter le port
De ces arbres, tes cris anciens, de pierre ou cendre.

Tu marcheras,
Tes pas seront longtemps la nuit, la terre nue,

Et lui s'éloignera chantant de rive en rive.

A UNE TERRE D'AUBE

Aube, fille des larmes, rétablis
La chambre dans sa paix de chose grise
Et le cœur dans son ordre. Tant de nuit
Demandait à ce feu qu'il décline et s'achève,
Il nous faut bien veiller près du visage mort.
A peine a-t-il changé . . . Le navire des lampes
Entrera-t-il au port qu'il avait demandé,
Sur les tables d'ici la flamme faite cendre
Grandira-t-elle ailleurs dans une autre clarté?
Aube, soulève, prends le visage sans ombre,
Colore peu à peu le temps recommencé.

UNE VOIX

Écoute-moi revivre dans ces forêts
Sous les frondaisons de mémoire
Où je passe verte,
Sourire calciné d'anciennes plantes sur la terre,
Race charbonneuse du jour.

Écoute-moi revivre, je te conduis
Au jardin de présence,
L'abandonné au soir et que des ombres couvrent,
L'habitable pour toi dans le nouvel amour.

Hier régnant désert, j'étais feuille sauvage
Et libre de mourir,
Mais le temps mûrissait, plainte noire des combes,
La blessure de l'eau dans les pierres du jour.

VENERANDA

Oh, quel feu dans le pain rompu, quelle aube
Pure dans les étoiles affaiblies!
Je regarde le jour venir parmi les pierres,
Tu es seule dans sa blancheur vêtue de noir.

Combien d'astres auront franchi
La terre toujours niable,
Mais toi tu as gardé claire
Une antique liberté.

Es-tu végétale, tu
As de grands arbres la force
D'être ici astreinte, mais libre
Parmi les vents les plus hauts.

Et comme naître impatient
Fissure la terre sèche,
De ton regard tu dénies
Le poids des glaises d'étoiles.

Apaisé maintenant, te souviens-tu
D'un temps où nous luttions à grandes armes,
Que restait-il
Dans nos cœurs qu'un désir de nous perdre, infini?

Nous n'avions pas franchi
La seule grille au soir ou sagesse de vivre
Qui est dans la grisaille et l'acanthe des morts.

Nous n'avions pas aimé
Le feu de longue nuit, l'inlassable patience
Qui fait aube pour nous de tout branchage mort.

LE PAYS DÉCOUVERT

L'étoile sur le seuil. Le vent, tenu
Dans des mains immobiles.
La parole et le vent furent de longue lutte,
Et puis ce fut d'un coup ce silence du vent.

Le pays découvert n'était que pierre grise.
Très loin, très bas gisait l'éclair d'un fleuve nul.
Mais les pluies de la nuit sur la terre surprise
Ont réveillé l'ardeur que tu nommes le temps.

DELPHES DU SECOND JOUR

Ici l'inquiète voix consent d'aimer
La pierre simple,
Les dalles que le temps asservit et délivre,
L'olivier dont la force a goût de sèche pierre.

Le pas dans son vrai lieu. L'inquiète voix
Heureuse sous les roches du silence,
Et l'infini, l'indéfini répons
Des sonnailles, rivage ou mort. De nul effroi
Était ton gouffre clair, Delphes du second jour.

ICI, TOUJOURS ICI

Ici, dans le lieu clair. Ce n'est plus l'aube,
C'est déjà la journée aux dicibles désirs.
Des mirages d'un chant dans ton rêve il ne reste
Que ce scintillement de pierres à venir.

Ici, et jusqu'au soir. La rose d'ombres
Tournera sur les murs. La rose d'heures
Défleurira sans bruit. Les dalles claires
Mèneront à leur gré ces pas épris du jour.

Ici, toujours ici. Pierres sur pierres
Ont bâti le pays dit par le souvenir.
A peine si le bruit de fruits simples qui tombent
Enfièvre encore en toi le temps qui va guérir.

La voix de ce qui détruit
Sonne encor dans l'arbre de pierre,
Le pas risqué sur la porte
Peut encore vaincre la nuit.

D'où vient l'Œdipe qui passe?
Vois, pourtant, il a gagné.
Une sagesse immobile
Dès qu'il répond se dissipe.

Le Sphinx qui se tait demeure
Dans la sable de l'Idée.
Mais le Sphinx parle, et succombe.

Pourquoi des mots? Par confiance,
Et pour qu'un feu retraverse
La voix d'Œdipe sauvé.

LA MÊME VOIX, TOUJOURS

Je suis comme le pain que tu rompras,
Comme le feu que tu feras, comme l'eau pure
Qui t'accompagnera sur la terre des morts.

Comme l'écume
Qui a mûri pour toi la lumière et le port.

Comme l'oiseau du soir, qui efface les rives,
Comme le vent du soir soudain plus brusque et froid.

L'OISEAU DES RUINES

L'oiseau des ruines se dégage de la mort,
Il nidifie dans la pierre grise au soleil,
Il a franchi toute douleur, toute mémoire,
Il ne sait plus ce qu'est demain dans l'éternel.